KNOTTY CONTOURS OF CIRCIMSTANTIAL EVIDENCE IN INDIA: SOLE BASIS FOR CONVICTION IN CRIMINAL TRIALS?

VOLUME 2, ISSUE 4 OF BRILLOPEDIA

MANOJ ARVIND P

Contents

Preface

"Start writing, no matter what. The water does not flow until the faucet is turned on".

• Louis L'Amour

Hundreds of students and professors are contributing their work to Brillopedia, we are here to provide ample information about Law and Contemporary issues. Our aim is to provide a platform for today's generation to express their views and ideas on law and contemporary law.

Author

Manoj Arvind P

CHAPTER ONE

ABSTRACT

It is axiomatic in the realm of law that a witness may lie but not the circumstances. Direct ocular evidence is not necessary for proving the person behind the crime. The guilt of a person can be proved by circumstantial evidence also. Four things are quintessential to prove guilt by circumstantial evidence: 1) That the incriminating circumstances pointing to the guilt of the accused must be well settled; 2) That the available facts must be in consonance with the hypothesis of guilt of accused; 3) That the circumstances must possess conclusive nature and tendency; 4) That the circumstances, should, to a considerable extent, eliminate every other hypothesis other than the one, proposed. However, both direct evidence and circumstantial evidence stand entirely on different footings in terms of the standards of proof, relevancy, admissibility and evidentiary value, which are required to be established. Emphatically, circumstantial evidence demands higher degree of proof vis a vis direct evidence as noted in the case of Pohalya v. State of Maharashtra, (1980) 1 SCC 530. In the case of Hidayat Ali v. State of Uttarakhand, 2022 SCC OnLineUtt 456, it was held that circumstantial evidence can be considered conclusive only when there is an established connection between the principal fact and the evidentiary fact in the issue. In a case, entirely reliant on the strength of circumstantial evidence, the burden on the prosecution is gargantuan when compared to the ocular evidence in case of direct evidence.

It is also settled that the accused cannot be convicted if the prosecution fails to establish the nexus in the chain of circumstances incriminating the accused. Also, motive of the accused bears immense significance in the cases relying solely upon circumstantial evidence. Most of the criminal cases are premised upon circumstantial evidence owing to lack of direct evidence in many a case. The question, which appertains consideration, is whether circumstantial evidence solely can form the basis for conviction in

a criminal trial or whether it requires any additional corroboration, which
needs to be examined in light of judicial pronouncements and several
underpinnings.

KeywordsCircumstantial evidence, Direct Evidence, Principal Fact,
Evidentiary Fact, Relevancy, Admissibility, Conclusive, Corroboration

CHAPTER TWO

INTRODUCTION

"For my own part, I think that if one were looking for a single phrase to capture the stage to which philosophy has progressed, 'the study of evidence' would be a better choice than 'the study of language'."[1]

The vigilant search for truth is the hallmark of our Criminal Justice system. The pursuit of truth is steered by evidences in criminal trials. Even the entire edifice of the Law of Evidence in India is concerned with setting out the guidelines as to "what facts might be utilized in evidence for choosing the disputed facts, how questioned facts are to be proved and what weight is to be attached to the facts illustrated as evidence" and so on. It is lucid that circumstantial evidence is a matter of indirect evidence which establishes the disputed facts through the establishment of other related facts in issue. In the case of Provincial Government Central Provinces and Berar v. Champalal, it was succinctly held that the non-appearance as a witness would be the strongest possible circumstance to discredit the veracity of the case. It is also settled that circumstantial evidence alone cannot form the basis for conviction since, in order for it to be admissible, it requires additional corroborative evidence. Nevertheless, even in the absence of direct evidence, courts have considered circumstantial evidence as the sole basis of conviction, if they are satisfied with the chain of conditions that demonstrates the guilt of an accused beyond reasonable doubt. These circumstantial facts are admitted as constituting a part of res gestae, i.e. it being a part of original proof of what has taken place. The sinuosity of this facet of our criminal jurisprudence will be exposited in this paper.

[1]AYER, ALFRED JULES, ALFRED J. AYERS, & A. J. AYER, PHILOSOPHY IN THE TWENTIETH CENTURY (London: Weidenfeld and Nicolson 1982).

CHAPTER THREE

MEANING AND AMBIT OF CIRCUMSTANTIAL EVIDENCE IN CRIMINAL TRIALS IN INDIA

At the very outset, it is to be acknowledged that a straitjacket formula can never be generalized to deal with all the cases sans any variance. Each and every case has to be gauged based on its own facts and in light of the evidence, furnished by the parties.[1] Not in all cases, the eyewitnesses or direct evidences are available to sustain conviction. In the absence of such direct evidence, circumstantial evidence brooks significance. Circumstantial evidence falls under the purview of indirect evidence, which relates to a series of facts to prove or disprove the facts in issue or factum probandum.[2] It is equally important to understand that circumstantial evidence does not establish the existence of facts directly, rather only via inference, through the proof of existence of other facts. More importantly, the circumstances out of which "the accused's guilt to be drawn must be established beyond reasonable doubt and should be shown to be proximately in nexus with the facts in issue or factum probandum".[3]

Moreover, in most of the cases, police officials rely upon circumstantial evidence to prove the charges in the absence of direct evidence regarding the same. In terms of evidentiary value, there is no distinction between direct and circumstantial evidence as suchbut the only difference lies in their approach in proving the crime, since the former directly establishes the crime, while the latter leads to an irresistible conclusion of guilt through the chain of existing facts or circumstances.[4] The onus on the prosecution, relying solely on circumstantial evidence, is heavier to discharge and the presumption of innocence of the accused should have a primary role in cases, which are based solely on circumstantial evidence.[5]

Under the statutory scheme of the Indian Evidence Act, 1872, ("IEA" hereinafter) intriguingly, the term 'circumstantial evidence' finds no mention. However as per the judicial literature, it can be betokened that the admissibility of circumstantial evidence is based on logical inferences in India. Both direct evidence and indirect evidence are at par if the whole linkage between the circumstances is unequivocally established per contra, if the factual chain is not complete, the accused is entitled to the benefit of the doubt[6] and the burden on the prosecution to discharge, will become heavier, in cases, which are premised solely upon circumstantial evidence.

A. Conditions to be satisfied

Particular rules of evidence have to be borne in mind, while dealing with the circumstantial evidence. The only shortcoming associated with circumstantial evidence, is that there is a grave likelihood of suspicion or conjecture taking the position of a legal proof, which should not be countenanced. To evade this, in our criminal jurisprudence, several principles have been laid down by the courts with regard to the appreciation of circumstantial evidence, which are seriatim.

As held in the case of SharadBirdichandSarda v. State of Maharashtra,[7]

"Firstly, the circumstances, which are relied on to frame the charges must be fully settled. Secondly, the facts, thus established, must be consistent only with the hypothesis of the guilt of the accused, that is, there should be no other explanation other than pointing to the hypothesis of the guilt of the accused. Thirdly, the circumstances, thus relied upon, should be of a conclusive nature and tendency. Fourthly, every other possible hypothesis should be excluded from consideration except the sole conclusion and fifthly, there must be completion in the chain of facts pointing to the guilt of the accused."[8]

The emphasis on these conditions for the admissibility of circumstantial evidence stems from the fact that, in any criminal case, whenever there arises any conflict between presumption of innocence of the accused and any other principle, the former will always prevail.[9] The very premise of circumstantial evidence is the undeniable causation which engenders satisfactory conclusion of guilt.[10]

The afore-canvassed conditions also have been cagily applied by the courts since time immemorial. It cannot be overlooked that the inference of guilt from a given set of circumstances would not itself suffice for consideration.[11] This is primarily due to the principle of proving the guilt of the accused beyond reasonable doubt, which is a cardinal principle in the Indian criminal jurisprudence.[12] This also does not imply that a single missing link in circumstances would sabotage the prosecution's case, rather, as long as the considered circumstances correlate with the factum probandum, the court will incline towards accepting the evidence.[13]

B. Legality of circumstantial evidence

It is vital to note that when the circumstantial evidence is solely relied upon, errors are bound to arise due to the problematic nature of circumstantial evidence or owing to human negligence. That is where the corroborative evidences like blood, fingerprint, DNA samples come into play, which must be preserved carefully to forge the connection in the chain of incriminating circumstances against the accused.[14]

Two contrasting views prevail with regard to the legality of circumstantial evidence. On one hand, circumstantial evidence is treated on par with the direct evidence. Per contra, it is notable that even the strongest circumstantial evidence cannot be admitted in court to prove the guilt of the accused. Equal footing is given to both direct evidence and circumstantial evidence in the US.[15] Pursuant to section 6 of the IEA,1872, circumstantial evidence constitutes the part of the same transaction as facts, which, although, are not factum probandum, are interlinked with a 'fact in issue', forming the part of same transaction. In a case, which is solely dependent on circumstantial evidence, the prosecution must be capable of elucidating with certainty the circumstances pointing to the guilt of the accused, for which the accused is charged.[16] The 'degree' of proof is the prime difference here. The incompatibility of all the incriminating circumstances with the innocence of the accused is the primary requirement for the legality and validity of circumstantial evidence.[17]

[1]Nagesh v. State of Karnataka, (2012) 6 SCC 477.

[2] SR MYENI, THE LAW OF EVIDENCE,20 (Hyderabad: Asia Law House 2007).

[3]SatishRajannaKartalla v. State of Maharashtra AIR 2008 SC 1184.

[4]MakbulAhammad v Abdul RahamanAkand, (1953) 1 Cal 348.

[5]Musheer Khan v State of MP, AIR 2010 SC 762.

[6]HarendraNarain Singh v State of Bihar, AIR 1991 SC 1842.

[7]1984 AIR 1622.

[8]SharadBirdichandSarda v. State of Maharashtra, 1984 AIR 1622

[9]Ashraf Ali v. King Emperor 21 CWN 1152.

[10] 4 B.W. JONES, EVIDENCE (5th ed.1947).

[11]*Sufficiency of Circumstantial Evidence in a Criminal Case*, 4 COLUMBIA LAW REVIEW 55, 549–60(1955).

[12]FerozPathan, Circumstantial Evidence: A Herculean Task for Prosecution, The Daily Guardian (Sept. 22, 2022, 2:20 PM), https://thedailyguardian.com/circumstantial-evidence-a-herculean-task-for-prosecution/.

[13]SatishRajannaKartalla v. State of Maharashtra AIR 2008 SC 1184.

[14]Ganesh Lal v. State of Rajasthan, (2002) 1 SCC 731.

[15]Holland v. United States, 348 U.S. 121,140(1954).

[16]State of Kerala v. Rasheed,2017 Cri LJ 3956(Ker).

[17]Venkatesan v. State of Tamil Nadu AIR 2008 SC 2369.

CHAPTER FOUR

A JIXTAPOSITION OF THE ADMISSIBILITY AND RELEVANCY OF CIRCUMSTANTIAL EVIDENCE VIS-AS-VIS DIRECT EVIDENCE

The question, which appertains to our consideration now, is whether direct evidence superior or inferior to circumstantial evidence. There are two polar opposite views on this. Firstly, it is popularly said that witnesses may lie but not the circumstances, thereby implying that circumstantial evidence is superior to direct evidence. This view is fallacious, since circumstances are just relevant facts which are placed before a court through a witness. But this logic could be extended actually to the direct witnesses too. Ergo, there is no reason for according primacy to circumstantial evidence over direct evidence. Actually, there is no difference in the probative value betwixt direct evidence and circumstantial evidence.[1]

Secondly, the view that circumstantial evidence is of lesser reliability than the direct evidence is also equally wrong. The circumstantial evidence, if put into use cleverly, can give greater argumentative value to steer the case in one's benefit.[2] Direct evidence, on hand, does not require any assumptions or suppositions to get a conclusion on the basis of available facts. Circumstantial evidence, on the other hand, fits under the expression "relevant facts" whose reliability is relatively high and difficult to suppress.[3]Conviction of an accused cannot be carried out solely based on circumstantial evidence if there is a break in the linkage of chain of circumstances against the accused.[4]To untangle this, light also has to be sourced from the fact of modern technological and scientific advances, which can be put into use for obtaining circumstantial evidence like the DNA evidence, fingerprints inter alia to assist the prosecution to secure the conviction of a criminal.[5] The circumstantial evidence has an edge over direct evidence in this regard since no malice or any other human frailties can be attributed to circumstantial evidence.

A. Operation and significance of 'motive' in the cases of direct and circumstantial evidence

The whole edifice of circumstantial evidence itself hinges upon the propinquity between the facts and circumstances in a given case. Motive,under section 8 of the IEA, brooks immense relevance in a case which is grounded solely on circumstantial evidence. It is well-settled that when direct evidence is available, the role of motive will be limited wherein the dearth or absence of motive may not influence the merits of the case. But when it comes to the case of circumstantial evidence, motive plays an important role in forging links in the chain of circumstances, which also needs to be proved beyond all reasonable doubt, otherwise the circumstantial evidence would not stand. The importance of the proof of motive cannot be understated in cases pertaining exclusively to circumstantial evidence.[6] Circumstantial evidence, howsoever strong it may be, if the motive is not established, will not be sufficient to convict the accused.[7]

The fragmented links in the chain of evidence and the non-establishment of proof of the case beyond a reasonable doubt, taint the circumstantial evidence which can be evinced through the following excerpt from a notable case:

""The milk which is said to be adulterated with the poison was taken out from the refrigerator, transferred into a pan for boiling, and thereafter given to the deceased. If it actually had organophosphorus in it the smell would have filled up the room. The deceased being a healthy woman aged 45 years would not have consumed it if the pungent smell was coming from the milk. Even the informant did not sense any foul smell from the milk while boiling it.""[8]

The factual matrix of the case can be briefly canvassed as: The allegation was that the wife of the informant died after consuming the milk supplied by the appellant. The informant maintained that the appellant had borrowed money from him and that his wife was doggedly demanding the same from him. Thus, on account of grudge, he poisoned the milk to eliminate his family. The trial court conceded to the establishment of circumstantial evidence and convicted the accused. On an appeal, the court, on the reappraisal of the evidence, found discrepancies in the laboratory reports, and the breakages in the chain of circumstances, and on the basis of the lack of motive, inter alia, ultimately exonerated the appellant.

It is also a settled proposition of law that the sole absence of motive cannot set aside the entire case of the prosecution. However, if the motive is established per se, it makes a direct link with the circumstantial evidence which will be irrefutable.[9]This testifies to the amorphousness of circumstantial evidence jurisprudence in our country.

B. Section 106 of the IEA, 1872-inoperative before the discharge of burden of proof by the prosecution

It is evinced that once the chain of events for the purpose of proving circumstantial evidence is established successfully by the prosecution, from which a reasonable inference is engendered against the accused, section 106 of the IEA will come into effect.[10] This section, although places the burden on the person who is having special knowledge of things, to prove the same, it, in no way, exonerates the prosecution from discharging its preliminary liability of proving the case beyond a reasonable doubt.

The unique thread that can be gleaned from almost all the Indian jurisprudence on the convictions based on circumstantial evidence is the integral role of 'motive',[11] since the "direct proof of intention is rarely available."[12] At the cost of repetition, it has to be flagged that in the appreciation of circumstantial evidence, the operation of motive, as can be evinced from the factual matrix, can very well serve as evidence,[13] in the absence of any kosher evidence to establish guilt.[14]

C. 'Suspicion', howsoever grave, cannot replace 'proof'[15]

It has been time and again emphasized that the court has to be cautious and avert the danger of a suspicion replacing a legal proof.[16] The courts are bound to conduct a voir dire to test the veracity and admissibility of evidence especially when the nature of evidence is circumstantial. Every criminal case is a nuanced travel from 'may be true' to 'must be true' and the entire travel distance has to be covered by reliable, legally kosher and unimpeachable evidence and not by suspicions and conjectures. It is also enunciated that in the absence of direct evidence, circumstantial evidence can premise the whole basis to convict.[17] Conviction, on the sole basis of circumstantial evidence, has to be examined further.

D. Reliability of circumstantial evidence: sole basis for conviction?

The prima facie answer to this question in the title, is in the affirmative as far as the Indian judiciary's approach so far, is concerned. Undoubtedly, convictions can be solely based on circumstantial evidence, but the caveat is that such evidence should be tested on the cornerstone of the law relating to circumstantial evidence.[18] Two landmark cases which are increasingly reliant on circumstantial evidence are the cases of PriyadarshiniMatoo[19] and Jessica Lal.[20] In the aforementioned cases, there was nary any direct evidence to implicate the accused. However, circumstantial evidence formed the sole basis for conviction, in the form of corroborative evidence to establish guilt thereby causing accused's conviction. The apposite question, to be asked, would therefore be, regarding the rules to be adopted in the appreciation of circumstantial evidence in conviction.[21] This case was anchored around the conviction for the offence of criminal conspiracy based on circumstantial evidence.

Section 9 of the IEA, 1872 validates the facts which settle the identity the accused as relevant.[22] Circumstantial evidence of identity rather than the testimonial evidence of identity is discussed under this section. Edwin Borchard argued that circumstantial evidence was "one of the prominent causes of wrongful convictions."[23] It is often emphasized that courts have suasponteduty to cagily examine the case when the prosecution relies entirely on circumstantial evidence to build their case.[24]

[1]Commonwealth v. Corriveau, 396 Mass. 319, 339, 486 N.E.2d 29, 43 (1986).

[2]*Sufficiency of Circumstantial Evidence in a Criminal Case*, 4 COLUMBIA LAW REVIEW 55, 549–60(1955).

[3]WILLS' PRINCIPLES OF CIRCUMSTANTIAL EVIDENCE (6th ed. 1937)

[4] Manipur v OkramJitan Singh, 2005 Cr. L.J. 1646.

[5]MR Zafer, Scientific Evidence-Expert Witnesses, Special Issue JILI (1972) 53.

[6] Babu v. State of Kerala, 2010 (1) KLT 132.

[7] Anwar Ali v. State of H.P., (2020) 10 SCC 166.

[8] Rajbir Singh v. State of Punjab, 2022 SCC OnLine SC 1090.

[9] Suresh Chandra Bahri v. State of Bihar 1995 Supp (1) SCC 80.

[10]SabitriSamantaray v. State of Odisha, 2022 SCC OnLine SC 673.

[11]Anil Sharma v. State of Jharkhand 5 SCC 679 (2004).

[12]Dr. KI VIBHUTE, PSA PILLAI IPC 204(14th ed. 2019).

[13]MunishMubar v. State of Haryana (2012) 10 SCC 464.

[14]Yunis v. State of Madhya Pradesh (2003) 1 SCC 425.

[15]Surinder Pal Jain v. Delhi Administration: 1993 AIR 1723.

[16] Jayaram v. State of A.P., 1995 Supp (3) SCC 333.

[17]Umedbhai v. State of Gujarat, 1978 AIR SC 424.

[18]HanumantGovindNargundkar and Anr. V. State of Madhya Pradesh,
AIR 1952 SC 343.

[19] Santosh Kumar Singh v. State, (2010) 9 SCC 747.

[20]SidharthaVashisht alias Manu Sharma v. State (NCT of Delhi),
(2010) 6 SCC 1.

[21] State v. Nalini, (1999) 5 SCC 253.

[22] Ram Babu v. State of Uttar Pradesh, (2010) 5 SCC 63.

[23] EDWIN M. BORCHARD, CONVICTING THE INNOCENT:
ERRORS OF CRIMINAL JUSTICE (The Justice Institute 2013).

[24] People v. Yrigoyen, 45 Cal. 2d 46, 49 (1955).

CHAPTER FIVE

CONTOURS OF 'LAST SEEN THEORY' AND ITS ADMISSIBILITY

The theory of last seen is one of the cardinal facets of circumstantial evidence, which helps in establishing the guilt of the accused thereby sustaining conviction. The bedrock of this theory is grounded upon probability as well as cause and connection, which is normally used when no other evidence can be obtained after the completion of investigation and when there is a presumption that the person, the deceased was last seen with, had a reason to commit the crime."[1]

False defenses can also be considered as a circumstance against the accused. False defenses taken by the accused charged of murder also constitute additional links in the chain of circumstances incriminating the accused.[2] The evidentiary value of the last-seen theory is immensely debatable. It is to be noted that even the last-seen together theory is inconclusive in nature in the absence of establishment of clear motive and proof of circumstantial evidences "beyond doubt". The case of Subhash Thapa v. State of Sikkim[3] bears relevance here.

The factual matrix of this case is that the appellant was charged with the murder of a man in a vicinity of half-kilometer from his home. Here, the prosecution dwells upon the 'last seen together theory' based on the testimony given by the police which is even debatable as he himself was travelling in a direction opposite to the place of occurrence of the crime. A fortiori, no motive attributable to the accused could be established by the prosecution owing to no personal connection of the accused with the deceased. In the cases, placing heavy reliance upon circumstantial evidence, the evidence must be so convincing to the extent where no other conclusion could be arrived at.

Adverting to the case of Anjan Kumar v. State of Assam,[4] where the accused was charged with rape and murder of the deceased. The deceased's severed body was found on a railway track after being last seen in one of the accused's houses. The HC held them guilty of causing death in furtherance of common intention as well as tampering with evidence under sections 302/304 and section 201 of the IPC respectively and the life sentence was awarded. Reliance was placed on postmortem report, blood samples as well as the notable last seen theory to create a chain of events to incriminate the accused.

The Court held that there was neither conclusive proof of corroboration of statement of investigation nor the blood stains on the weapons could be proved. In the absence of corroborative evidence, the last seen together theory alone could not sustain the conviction. Based on this, the HC's decision was reversed and the appellants were acquitted.[5]As far as the precincts of the last-seen together theory is concerned, two decisions bear significance. In State of UP v. Satish, it was observed as:

"22. The last seen theory steps into play where the time gap......being the perpetrator of the crime becomes not possible..."[6]

Even in such cases, courts have always been inclined to look for some corroborative evidence to uphold the conviction. When the entire case rests upon circumstantial evidence or last seen theory, the degree of proof required, is relatively higher.[7]The decision in the case of Nizam&Anr.v. State of Rajasthan, a ratio, which could possibly affect the very edifice of police investigation was held, which was that an accused could not be convicted merely because he was the last one to be spotted with the deceased particularly, "if a long time had passed between the sight and the time at which the murder was committed".[8]This last-seen theory does not operate in isolation and this theory is to be applied taking into consideration the case of the prosecution in its entirety by having regard for the circumstances preceding and the circumstances ensuing the point of being so last seen.[9]This decision would have immense repercussions on police investigations in tying up the circumstantial ends in cases, where the crimes are sensational, in the absence of eyewitnesses.

[1]Rohtash Kumar v State of Haryana, 2013 Cr LJ 3183.

[2] G Parshwanath v State of Karnataka, AIR 2010 SC 2914.

[3]Subhash Thapa v. State of Sikkim, 2021 SCC OnLineSikk 193.

[4]2017 SCC OnLine SC 622.

[5]Id.

[6] Satish Chandra v. State of M.P., (2014) 6 SCC 723.

[7] Manoharan v. State by Inspector of Police, 2006 SCC OnLine Mad 1235.

[8] Nizam v. State of Rajasthan, (2016) 1 SCC 550.

[9]Id.

CHAPTER SIX

CONCLUSIONS AND SUGGESTIONS

It is limpid that conviction based on circumstantial evidence or the last seen theory, connecting accused with commission of offence, should be proved beyond all reasonable doubt by the prosecution. Even if the Accused had failed to discharge burden under section 106 of the IEA, 1872, it would be irrelevant if the prosecution is unable to establish the chain of circumstances. Although, circumstantial evidence weighs a little lesser when compared to direct evidence in upholding a conviction, in the absence of direct evidence, convictions can even be solely based on the circumstantial evidence, and not otherwise. The question however here, is as to how far, the circumstantial evidences have been considered reliable and admissible by the Indian Judiciary. The doctrine of circumstantial evidence, although it finds no explicit mention in the IEA, 1872, is enshrined under section 6 of the IEA, 1872 wherein the relevancy of the facts constituting a part of the same transaction, is discussed.

The Indian Judiciary has long adhered to the approach that circumstantial evidence is not always needed to sustain a conviction, and that direct evidence need not always be there to prove a crime, owing to the impracticalities for the Police or other IOs in obtaining direct evidence, like eyewitnesses all the time.[1] Thus, the appreciation of circumstantial evidence, as the sole basis for convicting an accused is in itself a balancing exercise, wherein a delicate balance has to be struck between the societal interests of justice, at stake, in a given case, as well as the practical problems associated with gathering evidence for the police officials in proving a crime. This is purely a judicial exercise. These trials, based on circumstantial evidence, harp on the principle of Res ipsaloquitir. Such evidence, conclusively, required a greater degree of caution while appreciation, when compared to direct evidence.

[1] Kyle Anthony Zabbala v. People of the Philippines, G.R. No. 210760.